SIMPLY LOVE JESUS

CALEB S. DAVIS

D1211235

Simply Love Jesus
by Caleb S. Davis
Published by
Simply Love Jesus™ Ministries

Print ISBN: 978-1-7377814-0-0
Ebook ISBN: 978-1-7377814-1-7
Copyright © 2021 by Caleb S. Davis. All rights reserved.
www.simplylovejesus.com

Editing and Interior formatting by Ben Wolf
www.benwolf.com/editing-services

CONTENTS

INTRODUCTION

When I was nineteen years old, God put a question on my heart.

When I asked that question, I experienced a revelation; it was as if my entire life had changed. It changed the way I see people. It breathed new air into the way I understand truth. It revolutionized my faith. That question opened my eyes to something beautiful.

I believe this idea can breathe life into a movement that began over 2,000 years ago. The beauty of this question is that it doesn't actually come from something new; rather, it's about bringing many of us back to something very old, but in a new way.

It is my mission and purpose to teach others the meaning of this question. I want to share this same excitement, this same joy, this same way of living with you.

I'm honored to personally welcome you to this journey. I pray this book impacts you in the same way that one question transformed me.

How to get the most out of this book

My hope is not that you just read this book but rather that it would be one you *re*-read. I hope every time you open these pages, this book brings you back to some fundamental truths—the kind of truths that give you an extra kick you need to push through the hardships in life.

I pray that every time you read through this book it brings you clarity, helping push away the thorns and thistles that prevent you from seeing the road to wisdom.

I believe questions are powerful. I believe a really good question can completely shift the direction of someone else's life.

So whenever a question is asked in this book, don't just breeze by it.

Stop.

Reflect.

Actually put the book down, and ponder the question being asked of you.

I intentionally placed certain questions in this book that if you truly sit down and think about them, they can potentially unravel and entire new way of thinking for you.

Jesus once said this on the topic of worry:

> "Therefore I tell you, do not worry about your life, what you will eat; or about your body, what you will wear. For life is more than food, and the body more than clothes. Consider the ravens: They do not sow or reap, they have no storeroom or barn; yet God feeds them. And how much more valuable you are than birds! Who of you by worrying can add a single hour to your life?" (Luke 12:22-25 NIV)

Jesus calls us to ponder the birds. How many of us when

reading that passage actually stop and think about birds? Not many, if I were to guess. Yet we miss out on so much wisdom if we skip that simple step of stopping, slowing down, and thinking when we are invited to ponder a question.

So whenever you come across a question in this book, take time to think about it. Visualize the question. Paint a picture around it. Imagine the different outcomes of this question depending on how you answer it. Go back and forth and debate the question with yourself.

I believe in the power of good questions, and that's how this book is designed: it's filled with good questions, and it's intended to be *re-read*.

So as we embark on this journey, ask good questions. Don't feel the need to rush through this book. Take your time. You might miss out on a life-changing experience.

CHAPTER ONE

E verything is complicated. Or at least it seems that way, doesn't it? Friends, family, school, sports, politics, romance—the examples are endless.

Life was so much easier when I was a kid.

I would eat, play, and sleep. My problems were fewer in number.

But just like you, as I got older, life didn't continue to be all sunshine and rainbows. Hearts got broken, dreams were shattered, things didn't turn out as we expected.

For lack of better words, life got complicated.

When things get complicated, they can grow to be overwhelming. When something is overwhelming, it drains our joy.

And without joy, hope is increasingly difficult to find. The world needs a lot of hope right now, and maybe you feel you need some hope as well.

Everything is complicated. But Jesus is the one thing that shouldn't be. In fact, when we understand the answer to one question, all these complicated things in our world and in our lives will fall into place.

And this is that question: "What does it mean to simply love Jesus?"

I'm sure that by reading the name "Jesus" you might have some preconceived ideas. Sometimes I wonder how much people actually know who Jesus was.

You may know He's the central figure for Christianity. You may know He was a Jewish Rabbi who lived 2,000+ years ago.

You may even know that He said some famous things such as "Do unto others as you would have them do unto you."

But I wonder if, even for many Christians, there isn't much more beyond that.

Nobody Believes Something For Nothing

I wonder whether Jesus was nice, whether He was kind. I wonder what He valued, what He considered sacred. I wonder what made Jesus happy and what made Him sad. If Jesus were my friend, I always wonder what I can do to encourage Him.

Do you wonder about those things as well?

It's easy to only see people for their beliefs and ignore their humanity in the process. We often fall into the temptation to fixate on someone's position, and we forget that person is just that: a person.

They were once a child who grew up in a context filled with their own hardships. Their life experiences shaped what they value and why they think the way they think.

I think about whether we have done the same with Jesus. Some of us may believe we know what Jesus believes, but I'm not sure many people truly know why. I'm not totally sure many people truly understand who Jesus is as a person or know what He values and how that shapes what He thinks is best.

How many of us believe in Jesus but only because of what we were taught growing up? I wonder how many people would still follow Jesus if they actually knew who He is as a person, knew what He valued, and knew what He cares about.

In the same way, how many reject Jesus for His beliefs before trying to understand why He values what He values and who He is as a person?

Nobody believes something for nothing. Everyone has a reason, even God. Every person has a story filled with experiences and decisions that shaped them into who they are today.

You may be appalled by someone who is pro-this or anti-that, but I believe our polarization is rooted in the fact that you have not tried to learn who that person is. You haven't really tried to hear their story. You haven't really tried to know what, exactly, has led them to where they are today, what has led them to believing what they believe.

If you come up with a reason on your own, then you need to realize that *you* are contributing to the problem.

Everyone believes something for a reason. Everyone is where they are today for a reason, there's always a story behind the circumstance.

If we're not careful, prejudice can start here. Prejudice is birthed when we decide the *why* before we hear the story.

There's an impatience within us, and it leads us to where we don't ask questions, we don't try to understand; instead, we create an answer for ourselves.

Growing up, people would tell me not to give money to homeless people. I was told they would just use the money for drugs, that they are just lazy.

But no one actually knew that; it was an excuse. How could we be so arrogant to believe that we know what they're going to use that money for when we don't even know their name?

There's always a story behind the circumstance. This is why I say that prejudice is birthed when we decide the why before we hear the story.

We are tearing this world apart. But God wants to empower us to change this world, to be good stewards of what He has put in front of us. This includes the people God places in our lives.

Many people today reject Jesus, not because of who He is but because of how His followers portray Him. In the past 1,600 years, the Church hasn't exactly had a perfect highlight reel.

Incredibly corrupt and evil snakes have abused the identity of the *Christian* for their own selfish ambitions, resulting in generations of trauma and hurt inflicted on people who desperately need the beauty and acceptance of God's Kingdom.

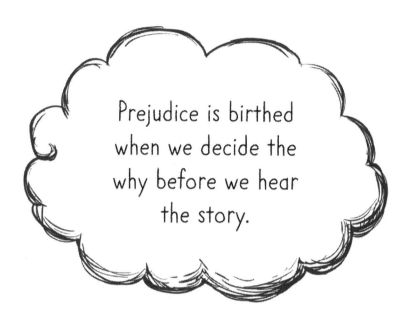

Prejudice is birthed
when we decide the
why before we hear
the story.

If you identify as a Christian, I need you to understand this: You are the world's first impression of Jesus.

What you say matters.

What you do matters.

The smallest and seemingly most meaningless of interactions matter.

You are the world's first impression of Jesus. And this world *needs* a good impression of Jesus.

This world doesn't need better lights, better music, bigger crowds, or a bigger stage. It doesn't need something that feeds the glutton for entertainment within every person.

This world doesn't need a new "movement." It doesn't need a new "spiritual encounter." It doesn't need a new spiritual "awakening."

This world doesn't need anything *new*; it actually needs something very *old*. It needs people who have been transformed from the inside out by the love of Jesus. And from *that* love overflows a sincere love for the people around them.

The world needs people who are loving, joyful, peaceful, patient, and kind. People who are good, faithful, and self-controlled. We need these gifts to be able to heal the brokenness in this world.

We need the greatest gift, love. "Three things will last forever—faith, hope, and love—and the greatest of these is love." (1. Cor. 13:13 NLT)

But what exactly is love?

Love is patient and kind, it does not produce pride or give selfish praise. Love is not rude. Love is not *me*-focused. Love is not easily irritated and does not hold grudges.

Love does not delight in injustice, immorality, and selfishness; rather, love rejoices in truth and goodness. Love never gives up; it keeps pushing forward. (1. Cor. 13:4-7, paraphrased)

Love is not complicated.

Love is not easy, but love is simple.

I believe this: Simple love has world-changing potential. The only way we can possess world-changing love is through a conviction that crucifies our "me-focused" nature.

A Great Big Beautiful Tomorrow

At the 1964 World's Fair, Walt Disney released the attraction now known as the "Carousel of Progress."

This attraction, featuring animatronics and rotating stages, highlights a family that steps through the decades with advancements in technology and home life.

Throughout this ride plays a song titled "There's A Great Big Beautiful Tomorrow," written by the Sherman Brothers.

I believe in a great big beautiful tomorrow. A tomorrow where believers follow Jesus the way He intended. A tomorrow where people would see Christians the way that God intended for them to be seen.

I'm not saying it'll be a world of sunshine and rainbows; our world may get a lot worse in some ways. But in the dark days to come, the Church will be the small but bright light that Jesus prays for us to be.

I believe that learning what it means to simply love Jesus plays a part in that vision. But again, it's not because this is something *new*; this is about bringing many of us back to something very *old*. I'm just presenting it in a new way.

My hope is that whether you believe in Jesus or not, you'll read with an open mind and an open heart. They can either change your life or enrich it in ways you won't expect.

"Simply Love Jesus" is an idea. It is a philosophy, a lifestyle. It helps make choosing *good* as something that is second nature. We don't have to *think* about it; we just *do* it.

SIMPLE LOVE HAS WORLD-CHANGING POTENTIAL.

Simply Love Jesus

Ever seen a movie where they start with the end and the rest of the film explains how we arrived at that ending? We're about to do the same exact thing. I want to lay it out for you, plain and simple. The rest of the chapters will explain how we got there.

This is a little different compared to many other authors. The ones I've read start by weaving pieces of their message together, and then, by the end, they reveal a brilliant tapestry showing how it all ties together. I want to go the opposite route.

There are four movements in this book, and each one naturally transitions us to the next one. All of them are motivated and fueled by the first. I call them "movements" because it reminds me of walking, which reminds me of a journey, which is what loving Jesus is like—a journey.

The first movement is called the *Question*.

The second one is *Know*.

The third is *People*.

The fourth is *Purpose*.

These aren't very sexy names for these "movements," but that's because they are keywords. Together, each of these keywords form a summary of *Simply Love Jesus*, which goes like this:

"Simply love Jesus" is the idea that everything should start and revolve around loving Jesus.

It starts with one *question*: "What does it mean to simply love Jesus?"

This question challenges me to love Jesus more because of what He has done for us. He first loved us by dying for us and rising from the grave so that we can have an abundant and eternal life. (Take a look at Romans 3:23, 6:23, 5:8, 10:9-10, 8:39, and also 1 John 4:10 and John 10:10)

THE FIRST STEP TO SIMPLY LOVING JESUS IS UNDERSTANDING THAT JESUS SIMPLY LOVES YOU.

The more I ask that question, the more I desire to *know* who He is. Just as a romantic relationship with someone requires me to intimately know them as a person, a true reflection of God's love will naturally lead me to want to know who God is. (1 John 4:16, 1 John 4:8.)

Not just as a sovereign King, Creator, Father, and Lord over everything, but as a *person* who unconditionally loves us. (Romans 8:39, Exodus 34:6, Lamentations 3:22-23, Psalm 136, Psalm 139:1-18)

I believe that by the power of the Holy Spirit, there are many ways we can learn who God is as a person. Three ways include prayer, reading and studying the Bible, and serving others.

The closer we are to Him, the closer He is to us. (James 4:8) The more we learn about who He is, the more we understand how to authentically love Him.

According to Jesus, Deuteronomy 6:5 and Leviticus 19:18 form one singular and greatest commandment:

"...love the Lord your God with all your heart, all your soul, and all your strength (mind)." (insertion added)
"...love your neighbor as yourself."

One of the greatest ways we can show God that we love Him is by loving *people,* and the Bible is clear that God loves all people. (Titus 2:11, John 3:16, 1 John 2:2, Psalm 86:5)

The more we authentically love God, the more sincerely

we will love other people—not just the people who believe in Jesus, but also the people who don't.

THE CLOSER I AM TO GOD,
THE GREATER MY LOVE FOR PEOPLE WILL BE.

This pursuit of loving others just as God loves us helps remind me of my *purpose* as a Christian: To love God with everything I have so I can love others and prepare the world for His imminent return. (Deut. 6:5, Lev. 19:18, Matt. 28:19-20, Rev. 22:20)

The reminder of my purpose as a Christian excites me about not only what God wants for us but also what He wants to do through us and how He desires to use us to make His plan for the world become a reality. (Rev. 21:1-4)

Recognizing this purpose helps me see how small I am in comparison to His holiness, but I'm equally joyful that He wants to include me in His plans.

I don't have what it takes to fulfill my purpose as a Christian through my own power, so I have to surrender to the reality that the only way I can do this is by relying on and being used through God's power.

THE MORE I SEEK JESUS
THE MORE I NEED JESUS.

To be empowered by God requires me to know Him.

To know Him requires me to desire Him.

To desire Him, I need to ask one question which sparks the never-ending cycle that this idea revolves around:

WHAT DOES IT MEAN
TO SIMPLY LOVE JESUS?

One time, as I was explaining to someone how God had changed my life with this question, they asked me. "So what *does* it mean to simply love Jesus?"

Answering that question took years of processing through it myself, but eventually I got there, and this book is the result of that process.

By the end of this book, we'll all be on the same page. You'll understand how God helped get me to this explanation of "Simply Love Jesus" and why it's so effective in helping us become the type of followers Jesus intended us to be.

With that said, let's get cracking! I'm so excited for us to embark on this journey together. If you haven't asked it out loud yet, why not start this book off strong? Ask the big question:

**WHAT DOES IT MEAN
TO SIMPLY LOVE JESUS?**

REFLECTION QUESTIONS

1. What feels complicated in your life right now?

2. Who is Jesus (to you)?

3. What do you think Jesus was like as a person?

4. What do you think a "Great Big Beautiful Tomorrow" looks like for our world? In other words, when you think of a perfect world, what does it look like?

5. What does it mean to simply love Jesus?

CHAPTER

TWO

THE FIRST STEP TO
SIMPLY LOVING JESUS
IS UNDERSTANDING THAT
JESUS SIMPLY LOVES
YOU.

Have you ever been in love? Had a crush, a bae, a boothang? After I graduated high school, I started an internship at the church I grew up in: Crossroads Church in Douglasville, GA.

During that time, we received a new volunteer. When I saw her, my fresh-out-of-high-school and hopeless romantic self had to do a double-take—she was beautiful! Butterflies invaded my stomach and started flapping around.

A mutual friend introduced us, and we instantly bonded over our knowledge of *Spongebob Squarepants* quotes. We spent the next couple of days messaging and calling each other. I sincerely wanted to know all about her. She was so easy to talk to, and I had so many questions!

What did she like to do for fun? What were her dreams? Did she like dogs or cats? What was her favorite candy?

And most importantly, does pineapple belong on pizza?

These were all cosmically important questions!

Even though things didn't work out in the end, it's funny looking back on it now. I probably looked silly, being so infatuated. But I wonder, how different would our relationship with Jesus be if we treated Him with such infatuation and wonder?

What would it look like to look silly for Jesus? Many Christians talk about having a personal relationship with Jesus, but how many of us make our relationship with Jesus *personal*?

Can a relationship with Jesus—with God—*be* personal?

In The Beginning...

According to believers, God is omnipotent (all powerful), omnipresent (everywhere, all the time,) and omniscient (literally knows everything.) Sounds like a pretty powerful dude, if you ask me. Yet Jesus invites us into a relationship with Him.

Here's some good news: God wants a *personal* relationship with you. In fact, this leads to the first step toward understanding the lifestyle we're discussing in this book.

THE FIRST STEP TO SIMPLY LOVING JESUS IS UNDERSTANDING THAT JESUS SIMPLY LOVES YOU.

Before we *do* anything, we have to ponder and meditate on what Jesus has already been *done* for us. We have to let His love for us influence our love for Him.

His love goes all the way back to before Jesus ever walked the Earth, before Christianity existed, before Judaism was established, before there were Israelites, before there were Hebrews, all the way back to the beginning of Creation itself.

Why the beginning? Because Jesus was there:

> "In the beginning was the Word, and the Word was with God, and the Word was God. He was in the beginning with God. All things were made through him, and without him was not anything made that was made." (John 1:1-2 ESV)

There's only one God whom I worship, and I believe He is *one* God. I believe Jesus is God. Yet I believe God the Father is also God. And there is also the Holy Spirit, who is also God.

I don't believe the God I worship is three "Gods" or that each is only one-third "God." They are all fully God, uniquely distinct, yet unanimously *one*. To better understand this, we can better understand the nature of God in one sentence:

> *The will of the Father is carried out by*
> *the obedience of the Son through the power of the Spirit.*

Confused? That's okay. Me too. But that's what makes it so mysteriously beautiful. I'll try to explain that another day, but I don't want to pull away from the focus of this chapter.

What I want you to understand is that Jesus's story doesn't start when He was born on earth as we are born, as a human. Jesus's story starts at the beginning of time itself.

In the beginning, God created the Heavens and the Earth. (Gen. 1:1) And on the seventh day, after He had finished His work, God rested. (Genesis 2:2). This creates the image of perfect unity and shared space in Creation between God and us. When God created humanity, He commanded them to be fruitful and multiply across the Earth.

God assigned humanity to work in cooperation with Him. They were supposed to reign over the Earth by imitating God and following His example as He governs the Heavens and reigns over us. (Gen. 1:28)

But instead of trusting His wisdom, we were deceived into being selfish, trusting in our own finite wisdom. Adam and Eve, the first humans God created, chose to disobey Him.

When that happened, a curse fell upon humanity and Earth—the curse of selfishness and evil: Sin entered the world. And it ruptured the relationship between God and humanity, between Heaven and Earth. (Genesis 3.)

The Power of Me

I'm telling you this because you need to understand that every issue goes back to the beginning.

All of your depression.

All of your anxiety.

All of your addiction.

Anything you may be struggling with all tracks back to that moment in the beginning.

All the crap in this world goes back to humanity's original sin. All the selfishness, the racism, the hatred, the poverty, the injustice, the suffering, the pollution—every issue in this world.

In order for what is wrong to be made right, we'd need to remove evil from the picture. But since that time, we have only shown that we cannot do this within our own strength.

God chose to be patient with us and allowed the passing of time to help teach this truth: we cannot fix the evil within our own heart and in our world through our own power.

All over the Scriptures, you'll see this phrase echoed: "Everyone did what was right in their own eyes." (Judges 17:6.) This is our fundamental problem with the issues in our world and in our personal life: Everything is *me*-focused.

It's always about what *I* want, what *I* need, what feels right to *me*. If something is broken, *I* have to fix it. If there's an issue, it's *my* problem. We try to overcome our struggles this way, how far does that get us?

When there are problems in the world, we're tempted to believe that everyone on social media needs to know *my* opinion on the matter. But opinions haven't done much to solve the world's problems.

Something within us compels us to trust in the power of *me*. Though we can't see it, it's that very desire that put this world in a cycle of evil and can drag us into its brokenness.

Romans 3:23 tells us that every person in this world has fallen short of God's glory. All people, because of what we as humanity brought into the world, are inherently selfish.

While you may be reading that and think, "I'm not selfish!" Let me ask you a question: When you were a kid, who taught you to lie?

No one. You just decided you did not want to get disciplined, so you lied.

This is our fundamental
problem with the issues
in our world and in our
personal life: everything
is me-focused.

Growing up, the living room in my house was the center of our home. In this living room, we had three brown leather couches. You could sit anywhere on these couches, *except* Dad's seat.

Dad would always sit on the couch that directly faced the television, and he would always sit on the seat farthest to the right. The leather cushion practically had his butt print formed to it. Any time someone was sitting there when he came to sit down, he would say, "Ah! Scooch! That's my seat."

Some of you may be reading this and know exactly what I am talking about. Even if you don't, you can probably figure out that there was only one seat in the entire house that I wanted to sit in: Dad's seat! Why? Because it was the one seat I was "not allowed" to sit in.

It's a silly example, but as silly as it is, it shouldn't be hard to realize that the primary issue in the world is that we are self-serving. You are no exception.

If you want the world's issues to change, it doesn't start by pointing fingers at someone else; it starts by taking a look at "the man in the mirror" as Michael Jackson once sang.

The selfishness and the evil within our hearts will drag us into brokenness, and that brokenness leads us to hopelessness. And when we dwell in a place of hopelessness, our enemy will place his checkmate.

John 10:10 teaches that the *thief* comes to kill, steal, and destroy. But Jesus came so that you could have life, and that you could have it abundantly.

What Is Sin?

At the beginning of this chapter, I brought up the idea of romantic relationships. Throughout this book, I will continue to use this idea as a running illustration. One thing you need to know about my story is that the pain of unfaithfulness is a theme that has run across my life.

I've suffered through multiple romantic relationships where the other person chose to be unfaithful.

I have persevered when unfaithfulness has affected my family.

I have endured when unfaithfulness affected the life and influence of my mentors.

I believe that cheating on a relationship is the deepest wound that one person could stab into the heart of another. The hurt it inflicts is excruciating, and the agony is nearly unbearable.

During college, I saw my selfishness in a completely new way. I was wrestling through personal struggles with pornography. The part that terrified me was that I wasn't feeling convicted about these struggles.

But it wasn't just a lack of conviction—it was a lack of *anything*.

I felt nothing.

I didn't feel bad, but I also didn't feel anything good, either. I felt no conviction, but I also felt no joy.

I felt *empty*. Not a sad emptiness, but beyond that, a true void of all emotion.

So I decided to do a deep dive into what sin was.

After several months of biblical, theological, and philosophical study (I'll spare you the long details of my homework), I came to a conclusion that shook me to my core:

Sin is the equivalent of cheating on a relationship with God

I knew the legal weight of sin, that God had paid a price so I could be set free. I knew the spiritual weight of my struggles, the tension between evil and good. I knew there were many important things to know surrounding the topic of sin and its relation between God and me.

But the moment I put evil—sin—my selfishness—into the idea of a relationship? It got *personal* quickly. But I suppose that's how Jesus wants it. He wants to make our relationship with Him personal.

The Scriptures teach us that all sin is not only a violation of a relationship but also a violation of the Law. This violation requires a payment to make things right. Because sin defies the very nature of God, who is life and breathed life into existence, the payment for these violations must be death. (Romans 6:23)

Romans 5:8 says that while you and I were *still* sinners, Jesus died for us. That is how God demonstrated His love. Instead of letting us pay the wages for our selfishness, Jesus took our place and chose to receive the death that we deserved.

Jesus allowed himself to be wrongfully murdered around 33$^{AD(CE)}$. He offered up His life so that through His historically monumental resurrection, three days later, we could receive everlasting life.

However, Jesus did not choose to die for me when I realized what I was doing was wrong. Jesus didn't die for me when I was on the ground, begging for forgiveness.

No, while you and I were *still* sinners, Jesus chose to die for us. While you and I were in the heat of the moment, wrestling under the covers with sin... when God was the *furthest* thing from our mind... *that* is when Jesus chose to die for you!

When I understood Jesus's love in this way, I fell facedown on the floor of my bedroom. Filled with remorse, I buried my face in my hands. And with tears streaming down my face, I cried out:

"I'm sorry!"

"I'm sorry!"

"I'm so, so sorry!"

"Father, please forgive me, I'm so sorry!"

I have endured the burden and the pain dealt by unfaithfulness, and it's something I would never wish on anyone else.

Psalm 78:40 and other passages in the Scriptures teach about how sin grieves the heart of God. I never took time to think about the fact that God still has feelings. He feels sadness. And it breaks His heart when we choose to be *me*-focused.

So to know that I am cheating on God—that I am throwing that type of hurt at Him every time I choose to live according to my selfish nature—it's absolutely heart-wrenching. I might as well have tried to pierce the heart of God... or maybe His hands instead.

The First Step

I don't know how much hurt I've thrown at God over the years. How much has God had to endure on my behalf, let alone the evil and selfishness throughout the history of the whole world?

Why would God endure and be so patient with all of us? Why would Jesus choose to die for us, despite all of the wrong we've done?

Well, among other equally important reasons, it's because Jesus simply loves you. If you can understand that Jesus simply loves you, that's your first step toward simply loving Jesus.

Philippians 2:6-11 and John 1:14 together teach us that Jesus gave up His divine privileges to come down from Heaven and make His dwelling among us. He paved the way for us to find truth and life by living in complete humility.

Because of this, we have seen the glory of the Father through His Son who was full of grace and truth. 1 John 4:10 is such a powerful passage. It teaches me that true love is not that we loved God, but that He *first* loved us and sent Jesus to die on our behalf.

Jesus simply loves you. If you can understand that, you can begin to know what it truly means to simply love Jesus. First, you have to believe it.

Believe that Jesus loves you.

Believe that He was alive and died for you.

Believe that He *is still* alive.

Believe that He is Lord, the highest authority over your life.

When you believe those things, you will never be alone again, because God's Spirit will always be with you. By trusting in Him, you are trusting in the power of the One who created the Heavens and the Earth.

Loving Jesus is simple, and I hope that by the end of this book you'll also believe this truth. Don't get me wrong: I'm not saying that loving Jesus is *easy*. In fact, sometimes loving Jesus is hard. I'm just saying that it is *simple*.

It's like running. Is running complicated? No. Running is simple. It's just putting one foot in front of the other at a steady pace.

But if you ask someone who just ran a marathon whether running 26.2 miles is hard, would they say yes? Absolutely. Loving Jesus is like that.

How do I remind myself to love Jesus, even when it's not easy? I ask a question: "What does it mean to simply love Jesus?" And I ask it *again*, and *again*, and *again*.

There's nothing mystical or supernatural about this question or the words in it, but for me it's a reminder. Every time that I ask this question, it serves as a reminder of everything Jesus has done for me to show me that He simply loves me.

Every time I ask this question, it sends me into a progression. It starts with God's love for me, demonstrated through how Jesus died for me so I would not perish but instead have an abundant and eternal life within God's Kingdom, through Jesus, and with God forever.

What's your story? Do you understand that Jesus truly loves you? Maybe even for the first time after reading these pages? This is how many people meet Jesus for the first time: by hearing the truth of what He did for us.

John 3:16 says that God loves the world so much that whoever believes in Jesus will not perish but have everlasting life.

I want you to take a moment and ask yourself that question: What does it mean to simply love Jesus?

Ask it again.

And again.

And again.

Ask it over and over and over. And when you do, think about your life. Think about where your life has come from, the story you've lived. Think about how, even if it was messy, God was still there.

The fact that it was messy means that God wants to do extraordinary things through you. He wants to use your messy story to reach other people who have messy stories.

Why does God allow us to have messy stories? Because this world is broken, and it needs people who sympathize with the brokenness. That through compassion we may be motivated to mend the wounds of others.

Wounds inflicted when we cheated on our relationship with God, caused by the selfish nature that infects the world and our hearts.

But the only way to mend these wounds is through the wounds of Jesus. That's why seven hundred years before Jesus was born, Isaiah foretold that it was by *His* wounds we are *healed*. (See Isaiah 53.)

Ask that question, and every time you do, let it remind you of these things. The first step to simply loving Jesus is understanding that Jesus simply loves you. That's what this question does: it reminds you that Jesus simply loves you.

REFLECTION
QUESTIONS

1. What does it mean to make your relationship with God personal?

2. Judges 17:6 says that everyone did what was right in their own eyes. How do you see this reflected in our world today?

3. "Sin is cheating on a relationship with God." What are your thoughts on this? How does it make you feel?

4. Toward the end of chapter 2, we read this:

"Think about where your life has come from, the story you've lived. Think about how, even if it was messy, God was still there. The fact that it was messy means that God wants to do extraordinary things through you. He wants to use your messy story to reach other people who have messy stories."

In the story of your life, what is messy?

5. Do you believe that Jesus is alive, that He died and rose again so that you could have life, and that God is the King of your life? Consider taking time to pray, talk to God, tell Him how you feel, and invite Him into your heart.

6. What does it mean to simply love Jesus?

CHAPTER

THREE

THE CLOSER I AM
TO GOD,

THE GREATER MY

LOVE FOR PEOPLE

WILL BE

What are you passionate about? Sports, music, video games, art? Humans are passionate creations: we love to put our whole heart into pursuing something that we care deeply about.

One of the things I love about Jesus is that He is passionate. He *loved* to learn and talk about God.

Around 62$^{AD \, (CE)}$, Luke, a skilled physician and a disciple of Saul of Tarsus, wrote a letter. (Saul is more often referred to as the Apostle Paul—Paul being his Greek name and Saul being his Hebrew.)

In this ancient letter, Luke compiled testimonies of other people who personally knew Jesus and lived during the same time He did.

Luke wanted to tell Jesus's whole life story and purpose so that the person to whom Luke was writing would believe and identify as a Christian.

Luke even interviewed people who knew Jesus as a little kid, which means he interviewed Mary of Nazareth, Jesus's mother.

What was it like raising Jesus?

I can't imagine, but what I think is so cool is that even as a child, Jesus was curious and passionate about His Father in Heaven:

"Every year Jesus's parents went to Jerusalem for the Passover festival. When Jesus was twelve years old, they attended the festival as usual. After the celebration was over, they started home to Nazareth, but Jesus stayed behind in Jerusalem. His parents didn't miss him at first, because they assumed he was among the other travelers. But when he didn't show up that evening, they started looking for him among their relatives and friends.

When they couldn't find him, they went back to Jerusalem to search for him there. Three days later they finally discovered him in the Temple, sitting among the religious teachers, listening to them and asking questions. All who heard him were amazed at his understanding and his answers. His parents didn't know what to think.

'Son,' his mother said to him, 'why have you done this to us? Your father and I have been frantic, searching for you everywhere.'
'But why did you need to search?' he asked. 'Didn't you know that I must be in my Father's house?' But they didn't understand what he meant.

Then he returned to Nazareth with them and was obedient to them. And his mother stored all these things in her heart. Jesus grew in wisdom and in stature and in favor with God and all the people." (Luke 2:41–52 NLT)

I absolutely adore that Luke notes that Jesus was sitting among the religious teachers, *listening* to them and *asking* questions.

What kind of questions did He ask?

Were they genuinely curious, or were they pointed?

Regardless, I believe His curiosity gives us something to think about.

God's Avocado Toast

In the last chapter, we discussed how the first step to simply loving Jesus is understanding that Jesus simply loves you. We can remind ourselves of this by reflecting on our story and how much God loves us.

But it shouldn't end there. Don't just think about how much God loves you and then leave it at that; rather, let it carry you. The purpose of reflecting on how much Jesus loves us is to create a desire within us. A desire to *know* who God is.

I love people, I really do. In fact, almost all of the entertainment I get really excited about is due to my friendship with someone else. Their excitement makes me want to experience that thing for myself.

I want to experience what excites my friends to deepen my relationship with them, to create a new point of connection between us. My favorite bands, video games, TV shows, and even foods can all be traced back to someone else.

Have you ever heard of avocado toast? One of my friends introduced it to me. She went on and on about how much she loves the avocado spread she puts on her toast in the morning.

This concoction involved taking avocados and mixing it in a bowl with "Everything But the Bagel" seasoning. Every other day, she spreads this avocado mix onto her multi-grain toast and then adds goat cheese to the top.

This, along with a fresh cup of coffee, sweetened with sweet cream creamer, is her breakfast.

Because she enjoyed it so much, I really wanted to know what it was about this avocado spread that was so tasty to her. So I decided to go to the store, hunt down the ingredients and make it for myself.

Now I rave about how good it is! If someone asks me for breakfast ideas, it's the first thing I recommend. It's easy to make, it fills you up, and it's *delicioso!*

I learned to enjoy avocado toast because my friend enjoyed it so much. And because I cared about her, I wanted to also enjoy what she enjoys and understand why she enjoys it.

I tasted it for myself and discovered that it was good. Our relationship with God should be the same. Psalm 34:8 says to taste and see that *the Lord* is good.

Will you discover God's avocado toast? He, like us, has stuff that He will go on and on about. Things that He loves and enjoys. But the question is, have you been paying attention?

The Bible is many things, and there are many people much smarter than I am who can teach you how to read the Bible the way that its various authors (who were inspired by God) intended.

But if there's one thing I want you to understand about the Bible, it's that the Bible is an opportunity to *know* who God is as a person.

How Far Are You Willing To Go?

As Jesus grew older, He continued to grow in His relationship with the Father. He often secluded himself to be alone just so He could pray. Jesus, even as an adult, still had a strong desire to know His Heavenly Father.

He was so passionate and dedicated that He often went

into the wilderness (Luke 5:16), even to the mountains (Luke 6:12), where He would spend hours upon hours praying. He would even regularly fast, depriving His body of food for a specific set of time, so He could allow God to sustain Him.

I tried to do a hardcore fast like Jesus once. It was not easy.

Jesus went forty days and forty nights without food. I tried the same thing.

I aimed for forty days and nights with *only* water. No food. I made it twenty-five days. I guess I don't have as much willpower as Jesus.

I broke the fast because my friend invited me over. His mom was cooking a bunch of chili. I ate fifteen bowls. Even after a bad stomach ache, it was still worth it!

In my fast, I honestly didn't learn a whole lot. I didn't come to some crazy revelation. The heavens didn't open up for me. It was just difficult, and I spent a lot of time reading and a lot of time praying and meditating.

Yet Jesus would *regularly* get out to be alone just so He could spend time with the Father.

Jesus desired to *know* who God is. He would sit in silence for hours, meditating, to listen and reflect on all that He knew about God so He could be closer to His Father. Spending hours alone with God was one of His favorite things.

How far are you willing to go to *know* who God is? Would you be open to not just know Him, but to be *known* by Him?

How far are you willing to go to know who God is? Would you be open to not just know Him, but to be known by Him?

He already knows you inside and out, but He wants you to experience being *known* by Him.

James 4:8 says that when we draw near to God, God draws near to us. One way you can draw near to God is through prayer.

Prayer is many things, but the simple version is that prayer is talking to God.

Our Father hears all our prayers. He hears everything we say to Him and desires for us to talk to Him—not just about things that we may want in life, but about *everything*.

You don't need to be in a specific place to pray. You can pray anywhere. In your home, in the car, at work or school—anywhere you are, the Father hears you.

Make it a habit to pray at all times and in every circumstance. The good, the bad, and the ugly.

Philippians 4:6-7 and 1 Peter 5:7 together tell us to cast all of our anxieties upon God, because He cares about us. When we do, the peace of God, which transcends all understanding, will guard our hearts and minds in Christ Jesus.

In case no one has ever told you this, God *cares* about you. He does, even if it doesn't feel like it sometimes. He wants you to have peace, and we realize that peace when we pray to Him.

Praying can bring us peace for many reasons, but one of them is because prayer brings us back to the truth—the truth of this world, how broken it is, and why things are the way they are.

And yet, despite things being broken, God refuses to give up and is in the business of reconciliation.

He refuses to just scrap everything. He wants us to have a chance at experiencing the Kingdom of God. So He sent Jesus to make a way to truth and life by *being* the way, the truth, and the life!

To Know and Be Known

When I dedicated my life to following Jesus, I owned a little pocket Bible. I kept it with me in my back pocket, and I took it everywhere I went. I wanted to know *who* God was. I wanted to know what He liked, what He loved, and I wanted to know who He is as a person.

So I read every day, every passing moment I had. When I was at a restaurant waiting for my food, I would pull out my pocket Bible and begin to read. When I was waiting in line at a store, I would read. When I was on vacation, I would read.

Whenever I finished reading the Bible, I started over. Sometimes I would switch to a different translation of the Scriptures, and I would re-read it from cover to cover. I finished a second time, and then a third time, and then a fourth time.

I read the Scriptures beginning to end seven times.

When I look back on that period, it reminds me of one of the most neglected books in the Bible, Song of Songs. If you've read it, it's easy to understand why many don't talk about it very much.

Song of Songs is a series of poems about a young woman and a shepherd boy who are madly in love. To be frank, they're also pretty horny for each other. The poems consistently illustrate how they desire each other in *every* intimate way.

Honestly, many Christians don't talk about this book, but we shouldn't neglect it. I believe this ancient, poetic, sexy romance novel serves as a wonderful illustration not only for passionate romance and how beautifully God created us to desire that, but it also helps us have a more passionate relationship with Jesus.

It can help us realize that God's love for us is *even deeper* and more enriching, and that in this world, through romance, we can get a small taste of the intimacy and eternal joy and completeness described in that book.

These feelings, longings, and wantings should serve as a reminder to desire God, to *know* who God is. In the third chapter of Song of Songs, look how the character of the young woman desperately desires her lover:

> "All night long on my bed
> I looked for the one my heart loves;
> I looked for him but did not find him.
> I will get up now and go about the city,
> through its streets and squares;
> I will search for the one my heart loves." (Song
> of Songs 3:1-2 NIV)

How far are you willing to go to *know* who God is? Would you be open to not just know Him, but to be *known* by Him?

Look how in turn, the young man in this poem also longs to intimately be with his lover.

> "You have stolen my heart, my sister, my bride;
> you have stolen my heart
> with one glance of your eyes,
> with one jewel of your necklace.
> How delightful is your love, my sister, my
> bride!
> How much more pleasing is your love than
> wine,
> and the fragrance of your perfume
> more than any spice!" (Song of Songs
> 4:9-10 NIV)

(Side note: "my sister" in this poem does not mean a literal biological sister. This was an allegory to express closeness. Meaning, a sister is a sister forever. So he desires to have her forever as his bride. We use this term similarly today when we have friends that are so close we would say they're like "brothers" or "sisters.")

When we draw near to God, God draws near to us. He wants you. He desires a relationship with His creation.

What are you waiting for? If you feel that longing that says "*Yes!*", then go! Go and *know* who God is.

God wants you to know who He is. He wants you to love Him with all of your everything. I'm serious—if you're feeling it, put down this book, trade it for a Bible, and just dive into the Scriptures for a while!

The Bestest Command

When I was maybe four years old, I remember arguing with my twin brother over which Disney movie was the best. He told me that his favorite was the "best" and I remember arguing that my favorite was the "bestest."

Probably not the most convincing argument, but in my head, "bestest" beat "best," and that's just how it was. You can't beat the bestest because it's the bestest.

With that being said, what's the bestest command? I know when you try to start reading the Scriptures, it can feel like a lot. The Scriptures are complicated—or at least it seems that way, doesn't it? But did you know we can actually simplify all of the Scriptures down to *one* command?

Jesus once said, "Truly, I say to you, unless you turn and become like children, you will never enter the kingdom of heaven." (Matthew 18:3 ESV) It's important when opening our minds to knowing who Jesus is to remember that sometimes we have to just approach it with the simplicity of a child.

Thankfully, we can spend our entire lives seeking to understand the vast wealth of Scripture. But at the same time, we only need to understand one bestest command to give us the right filter.

In the book of Deuteronomy, Moses and the Hebrews were in Moab. Moses knew his time was coming to an end. He wanted to deliver his last words to the people entering a land promised by God to their forefather Abraham, and now also promised to them. In chapter 6, Moses says these words:

"Hear, O Israel: The Lord our God, the Lord is one. Love the Lord your God with all your heart and with all your soul and with all your strength. These commandments that I give you today are to be on your hearts. Impress them on your children. Talk about them when you sit at home and when you walk along the road, when you lie down and when you get up. Tie them as symbols on your hands and bind them on your foreheads. Write them on the doorframes of your houses and on your gates." (Deuteronomy 6:4–9 NIV)

You might recognize one of those verses that I quoted: "Love the Lord your God with all your heart, and with all your soul and with all your strength." That's Deuteronomy 6:5, and Jesus quotes it when He was asked what the *greatest* commandment is.

Personally, I believe many of us have a very vague and shallow understanding of the "greatest commandment." I believe many Christians usually think of it as constrained to just Deuteronomy 6:5. But it's so much more than that.

In fact, Jesus takes two commands and slaps them together as one *singular* and bestest (or greatest) commandment. We'll get to that in Chapter 4.

These days, love can be vague and subjective. But when Jesus was asked what the greatest commandment is, He starts with this passage, and the Jews would have known it very well.

In Judaism, Deuteronomy 6:5 is part of Deuteronomy 6:4-9, which they refer to as Shema Israel (or *Sh'ma Yisrael*; Hebrew: שְׁמַע יִשְׂרָאֵל; "Hear, O Israel") or "The Shema" for short.

This passage is the most sacred prayer in Judaism. Still to this day, some Jews pray this passage twice a day, in the morning and evening.

In order to properly understand what Jesus meant when He quoted Deuteronomy 6:5, we need to understand it within the context of the Shema.

Jesus was, and is, a Jew. We have to get into the worldview of the Jews to see scripture the way they saw it. And they saw it within the full context of Deuteronomy 6:4-9.

Let's say someone is infatuated with you and has a crush on you. But let's also say that person comes up to you and says, "I want to talk to you every day. When you get up, when you go to bed, when you're at home or away. When you're with your family, when you're alone. I want to talk to you every second of every single day for ever and ever!"

Cue the creepy stalker violin from the movie *Psycho*, because that person is obsessed!

Yet that's exactly what Jesus is calling us to do: Jesus wants us to make God the object of our obsession. With all your heart, love Jesus. With all your soul, love Jesus. With all your mind and all your strength, love Jesus.

With all of your everything, love Jesus.

That last sentence sounds a little childish to me, but I kind of like it that way. When I was a kid, I believed anything my dad told me. I was that kid who, if you argued with me, my answer to being questioned was, "Because my dad said so!"

I wonder... what it would look like for us to view this command with such childlike love and faith?

When you're on the road or home, what are you talking about? Loving God.

What are you teaching to others? Love God.

When you lie down or when you get up, love God!

What are you binding on your hands and forehead? A reminder to love God!

Write it on your doors and windows, everywhere you go and everything you do: With all of your everything, love Jesus!

In one sense, we should make it that childish: simply love Jesus. Why? Because Dad said so. But also because God loves us so much and is so trustworthy. He has always been there for you and with you in every season, even the hard ones.

He pursues you, He longs to have a relationship with you, He desires to mature you and grow you like a father raising a child. We should long to love Jesus.

Don't ignore that longing. Let God's love for you fill you up and make you just want to shout with excitement and leap with joy!

If you don't think Jesus is exciting, then you haven't been spending enough time with Jesus.

But it's up to you to discipline yourself to spend time with Him. Sometimes, it's easy. Some days you just have the longing deep in your soul, so you have to drop everything you're doing and just read the Scriptures.

On the other hand, some days we just don't feel it. I get it. Some days we don't long for it. We feel like doing other things at the moment. It can be difficult, especially when life hasn't been kind to you.

Whether you feel like seeking Jesus or not, I promise you this: Jesus is never convenient. Something else will always try to fill your time. A relationship with God is a joy, but it's also a discipline.

What should you do when you don't feel like drawing near to God?

I ask a question: "What does it mean to simply love Jesus?"

Why? Because when I ask that question, it reminds me of His goodness and His grace.

It reminds me that He came, died, and rose again so I could be liberated from the selfishness within me that causes brokenness. It reminds me that He wants to empower me to change the world, even though I'm just an ordinary person!

That question brings me back to the Gospel and rejuvenates my spirit, and then I'm ready to dive right in to pray or read scripture! In the same way, whether it's asking that same question or something else, you have to discover what will bring *you* back to the Gospel and rejuvenate *your* spirit.

What truths do you need to re-hear over and over again? Which truths will ignite a fire in your spirit the more you preach them to yourself? And when you have that fire ignited again, how will you draw near to God?

Dive into the scriptures, pray, sit down outside, and just slow down—look at nature, reflect on it, think about how God spoke all of it into existence. Why did He want trees to grow the way they do? Why is the sky blue? How deep is the ocean? Can any of it teach you more about yourself in relation to God?

How far are you willing to go to *know* who God is? Would you be open to not just know Him, but to be *known* by Him? The Bible is an opportunity to know who God is as a person. And the more that you and I get to know Him, one thing should become obvious: God loves people.

REFLECTION
QUESTIONS

1. What are you passionate about?

2. How far are you willing to go to know who God is?

3. What does it mean to you to be known by God?

4. Read Matthew 18:3, what do you think it means to have the faith of a child?

5. Reading the Bible is a great way to know who God is as a person, but there are some days that we just don't feel like it. What should we do to help us during times like these?

6. What does it mean to simply love Jesus?

God's Avocado Toast:

Ingredients:

- 2 pieces of Sourdough bread (toasted)
- 1 Avocado
- Goat cheese
- Cilantro (chopped)
- Everything But The Bagel Seasoning
- Honey

*servings of cheese, cilantro, seasoning, and honey are subjective to your preference of taste

Directions:

1. Toast bread.

2. While bread is toasting, mix avocado up in a bowl with a spoon until it is a smooth paste. (Or leave it a little chunky, if you like it that way!)

3. Add seasoning and chopped cilantro to avocado and mix together.

4. After bread is finished toasting, spread avocado mix on to bread slices.

5. Spread goat cheese on top of avocado mix

6. Light spread of honey in zigzag motion.

7. Enjoy! Psalm 34:8

CHAPTER

FOUR

THE CLOSER I AM
TO GOD,

THE GREATER MY
LOVE FOR PEOPLE
WILL BE

I hope that by this point in our time together, your relationship with Jesus has been enriched. I hope you've taken time to sit back and reflect.

Maybe that means sitting on a porch with a drink in hand for a little while. Perhaps you're listening to the singing birds of spring or the buzzing from the summer cicadas. Maybe it's watching the warm falling colors of Autumn or feeling the brisk cold air of Winter's morning.

Every time of year is a good time to sit and think about Jesus, because Jesus should be involved in every season of our lives.

To summarize what we've talked about so far: The first step to simply loving Jesus is understanding that Jesus simply loves you. To remind ourselves of this, we can ask a question: "What does it mean to simply love Jesus?"

The more we ask that question, the more it should stir in us a desire to know who God is as a person, because it brings us back to what Jesus has done for us and reminds us of His amazing unfathomable love.

We can know who Jesus is through many ways, two of which are through prayer and the Scriptures. Prayer can be many things, but the short version is that it's the process of talking with God. Take time to sit alone, or even with others, and dedicate time to talk to God and listen to Him.

We can also know who Jesus is by reading the Scriptures. The collection of poems, autobiographies, letters, and other pieces of ancient literature that God inspired His people to write.

He did this so we could meditate on them and discover His grand narrative and plan not just for the world, but also for you.

When we dive into the Scriptures, this should be very obvious: God cares about people.

Good News!

When Jesus was thirty years old, He set off to travel and speak to people about what He was passionate about. His mission was to proclaim the Gospel (which means "good news").

According to Jesus, the Gospel is that, "The Kingdom of God is near" (See Mark 1:15.) We'll talk more about this mission and purpose in the next chapter, but one side of understanding this good news is that we are never too far gone, God will always pursue us.

Several hundred years before Jesus walked the Earth, the Jews were living away from Jerusalem in exile for their disobedience against God. They believed that their rebellion and their pursuit of selfish desires had made them irredeemable, that God had turned His back on them.

How many of us have ever believed that we were too far-gone, that we've messed up *too* badly? Maybe it was with your significant other, or you seriously hurt a friend, or perhaps you damaged your relationship with your parents.

Many of us have felt the weight of fearing we were too far-gone. When we look at our life with the perspective of what the Scriptures teach about Jesus, we can easily feel that we're *too* messed up for Jesus, that God looks at us with disappointment.

However, here is some *good news*: God does *not* see us as too far-gone. Rather, He continues to pursue His people. When the Jews believed they were too far-gone, God empowered specific people to share His word with them, to encourage them that there is *good news*: God is coming soon.

He had not abandoned His people, and they were not too far-gone. In fact, one day, God's Kingdom would spread across the entire world, and all people would get to share in it (Isaiah 40), all of it would be ushered in by the *Messiah* (which means "Anointed One").

No matter how bad things may be, God will always pursue you. He desires to see all things made right. So it was *the will of the Father* that a little over 2,000 years ago would be the proper time to send the Messiah. The "Anointed One" would usher in the Kingdom that the Jews were waiting for with great anticipation.

But God did something the Jews didn't expect. Not only did God refuse to turn His back on the Jews, but also the very Messiah who would usher in God's Kingdom was *God* Himself. The Son carried out the will of the Father, pursuing people.

Why? There are many reasons, but one of them is because Jesus simply loves us.

God loves you, and He refuses to give up on you. Even when you're at your worst, God will love you with His very best.

Jesus's disciples perfectly revealed this by detailing the types of people that Jesus spent His time with. One of my favorite stories about Jesus was when He went over to Samaria and talked with a woman at a well.

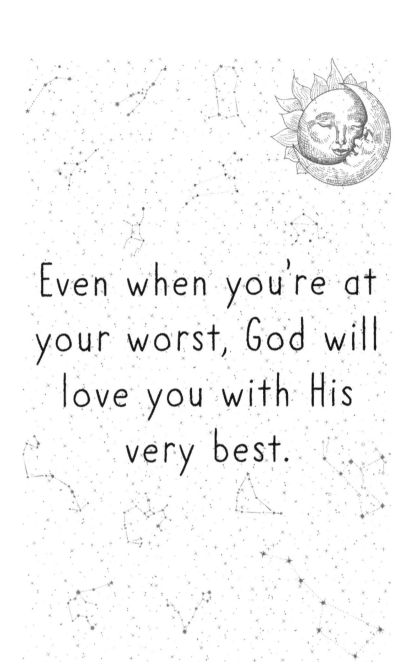

Even when you're at your worst, God will love you with His very best.

Samaritan Mudbloods

The main thing you need to know about Jews and Samaritans is that they did *not* get along.

Like, at all.

Their history of prejudice went back seven hundred years. We could spend a long time on scholarly and biblical explanation, but I imagine you want to keep things simple and get straight to the point rather than watch me get all nerdy.

As it happens, I believe the *Harry Potter* series by J.K. Rowling serves as a great illustration to better understand the tension between Jews and Samaritans. For those who have read or watched the *Harry Potter* series, the Jews (in this context) would be *Pure-Bloods*, and the Samaritans were seen as *Mud-Bloods*.

For those who have not seen or read this fictional series, allow me to explain a little. I'll go ahead and say that if you do not think someone should read or watch this series, I respect your opinion. I just believe it serves as a great and modern illustration that many readers will understand.

In the wizarding world of Harry Potter, everything centers around magic. Humans are classified into two categories: People who have magic in them (Wizards/Witches) and people who do not have magic in them (Muggles.) Within this novel series, J.K. Rowling wanted to create a fictional parallel to the extreme racial prejudices that infects our world today.

So in *Harry Potter*, groups of Wizards and Witches believe that those who do not possess any non-magical ancestors in their family are superior. They are called *Pure-Bloods*. Meaning, pure magical blood.

Despite being both humans, these types of people saw non-magical humans as having "dirty blood;" they saw them as less than human. And so, these extremists developed a derogatory term for wizards or witches who have muggle parents: *mudbloods*.

This is similar to how Jews viewed the Samaritans. Samaritans were Jews who, over seven hundred years prior, settled in the region that would come to be known as Samaria and intermarried with non-Jewish people groups. So the Jews who returned to Jerusalem after the Babylonian Exile saw them as half-breeds, less than human, people who had "dirty blood."

Okay, back to one of my favorite Jesus moments. He goes into Samaria and stops at this very famous well belonging to His ancestor Jacob. Then this Samaritan woman shows up to draw water from the well.

Jesus asks if she would draw some water from the well for him. She is surprised, and who wouldn't be after getting an idea of the prejudice between Jews and Samaritans?

However, Jesus intentionally guided this conversation. He responds and tells her that if she knew who He was, she would instead ask *Him* for water and know that He would give her eternal water.

"Jesus answered, 'Everyone who drinks this water will be thirsty again, but whoever drinks the water I give them will never thirst. Indeed, the water I give them will become in them a spring of water welling up to eternal life.'" (John 4:13-14 NIV)

Now, let's pause for just a moment. Although Jesus was speaking specifically to the Samaritan woman, His metaphor serves as a powerful lesson for you and me.

To get water from a well, you have to bring a bucket. You have to lower it down into the well. And using your strength, you have to pull up the water to provide for yourself. This kind of water will always leave a person wanting more.

How many of us try to overcome our struggles this same way? "It's *my* problem, so *I'll* fix it." We think we have to possess the power to overcome the issues in our relationships, in our lives. We think we have to wield the strength to overcome the problems that we see in the world around us, through our power.

But according to Jesus, if we follow the illustration of the water: Anyone who drinks from the water that we can produce by our own effort will always leave us thirsty again. But if we receive the water that comes from God's power and not our own, we will *never* be thirsty again.

You are the enemy to your own victory. The best thing that you can do in the battle against your struggle is to let go and let His power be your source of strength. Put all of your energy in keeping your eyes fixed on Him and on the mission of sharing God's love with the people around you who are in need.

Not Rejected

Getting back to Jesus and the Samaritan Woman—when Jesus tells her that if she takes the water He offers, then she would never thirst again, she takes Him literally and desperately asks where she can get this water so she'd never have to come back to this well again.

In response, Jesus asks her to go and get her husband. She then explains that she has no husband. Jesus then informs her that she has actually had five husbands in the past, and the man she lives with now is not her husband.

There was literally no way for Him to know that. But through the power of the Holy Spirit, He knew everything He needed to know to steer this conversation to tell her about the Good News of God's Kingdom.

Here's how the rest of that conversation turned out:

"Sir," the woman said, "I can see that you are a prophet. Our ancestors worshiped on this mountain, but you Jews claim that the place where we must worship is in Jerusalem."

"Woman," Jesus replied, "believe me, a time is coming when you will worship the Father neither on this mountain nor in Jerusalem. You Samaritans worship what you do not know; we worship what we do know, for salvation is from the Jews. Yet a time is coming and has now come when the true worshipers will worship the Father in the Spirit and in truth, for they are the kind of worshipers the Father seeks. God is spirit, and his worshipers must worship in the Spirit and in truth."

The woman said, "I know that Messiah is coming. When he comes, he will explain everything to us." Then Jesus declared, "I, the one speaking to you—I am he."

(John 4:19–26 NIV)

Afterward, the Samaritan woman runs through the town proclaiming that Jesus could be the Messiah, and many Samaritans heard and believed His message because of it.

This woman, who was rejected by her community because of her many marriages, who was rejected by the Jews because she was a Samaritan, was *not* rejected by God.

When Jesus met her, she was at her worst. She'd been through five disastrous marriages, and she wasn't even married to the man she was living with. Yet even when she was at her worst, God loved her with His very best.

She was the very first person to whom Jesus verbally confirmed that He was the Anointed One (Messiah), who ushers in God's Kingdom, and he made sure she knew she wasn't too far gone.

The same is true for us: None of us are too far gone. Even when you are at your worst, God loves you with His *very* best. The question though, is will we show the same kind of love and acceptance to others as Jesus did to this Samaritan woman?

The Bestest Command (Part 2)

In chapter three, we mentioned how Jesus was once asked what the greatest commandment is. Jesus answered that question with two passages of Scripture:

The first passage is Deuteronomy 6:4, "Love the Lord your God with all your heart and with all your soul and with all your strength."

The second passage comes from Leviticus 19:18, "...love your neighbor as yourself."

Jesus uses these two commands to form *one* greatest (bestest) commandment.

I believe Jesus does this to communicate to everyone an

important message. He wants us to understand that our relationship with God is reflected in our relationship with the people around us. Not just the people we agree with but also the people we don't.

If you take the time to read through the life of Jesus according to the Scriptures, (which you totally should, if you haven't yet!) everything Jesus teaches and does points back to that idea—even the way He taught His disciples to pray.

Have you ever heard what many refer to as *The Lord's Prayer*? I personally prefer the old-school version. It's nostalgic for me. It goes like this:

> "Our Father which art in heaven, Hallowed be
>   thy name.
> Thy kingdom come, Thy will be done on earth,
>   as it is in heaven.
> Give us this day our daily bread.
> And forgive us our debts, as we forgive our
>   debtors.
> And lead us not into temptation, but deliver us
>   from evil:
> For thine is the kingdom, and the power, and
>   the glory, forever. Amen."
> (Matthew 6:9-13 KJV)

I find it so fascinating that in Jesus's original example of prayer, half of it is dedicated to God, and the other half is dedicated to people.

It was very common where I grew up to believe that as long as you went to church every Sunday then everything was okay. It didn't really matter if churchgoers gave money to the homeless, or served other people, or were even kind to others for that matter.

As long as you went to church, and maybe read your Bible occasionally, prayed at your meals, then you and God were good to go.

But what Jesus wants you to understand is that if you and the people around you are not good, then you and God are not good. If the way you treat the people around you is not selfless and reflective of the generous love God shows us, it shows that you're not as close to God as you may think.

When God finished all He had created in six days, with humanity as the pinnacle of His Creation, He said it was *very good*. And on the seventh day, God rested. (Genesis 1:26-2:2) Everything was perfect. But then things got messed up, and it made God angry. Rightfully so.

But you know what? God continued to be faithful and love people. Why shouldn't we? There's a difficult question that has to be answered, and I'm sure you're already thinking it:

How can I love people who are unlovable?

Or, put another way, how can I serve people whose lifestyle does not honor God?

The Second Step

It's not complicated: simply love Jesus. When you and I have a hard time loving the people in front of us, it's because we're seeing them through our hearts, through our reasoning, and through our sense of justice.

Instead, we should view people through the heart of God, with a heart abounding in love, gracious and merciful, and slow to anger. The more we see people through the love of Jesus, the more clearly we see how to serve them.

The first step to simply loving Jesus is understanding that Jesus simply loves you. The second step is understanding that *the closer you are to God, the greater your love for people will be.*

The more you seek to know who God is as a person, and the more quality time you spend with Him, the more your love for human beings will also grow. As your relationship with God grows, you'll begin to care about the same things He cares about.

Let me tell you how big tips and lots of tacos led to a conversation about Jesus.

In January of 2018, I moved to Iowa to pastor high school and middle school students for Westwind Church. In Iowa, I had no family, no friends, the only person I knew was my boss, Jason.

Though the reason for my move was pretty unprofound, God had taught me many profound lessons. One of these lessons was seeing how simple loving people can be.

At the time, I lived in a one-bedroom apartment in a popular area of town. One establishment, in particular, not only sold really good food but also—how do I put this— "adult beverages."

The first time I visited this place was for lunch. I sat down, and a waitress introduced herself and asked what I'd like to eat or drink. I asked what she would recommend.

She began to brag on how good their chicken wings were. I was sold and I ordered myself some (and they were indeed, very good.) A week later I came back, and I had the same waitress. I remembered her name, and then I asked how she was doing.

"Good," she replied.

"No, how are you really doing?" I pressed.

She proceeded to tell me how if she were honest, she was pretty stressed out: she had a job interview coming up, plus, she'd had some pretty rude customers throughout her day.

All I did was listen. At the end of my meal, I wanted to make sure she had at least one good smile on her face. So for a

$12 meal, I left a $20 tip. Why? Because I wanted her to know that I simply cared about her.

I continued to visit that restaurant, and I requested the same waitress. The more that I visited, the more I got to know other employees as well. After a couple months, people would recognize me and address me by name when I walked in. I continued to encourage them, listen to them, and leave good tips.

A lot of these employees would work from 4:00pm to 2:00am. Some of them would work with no breaks. I saw a need to be met, and these people had become my friends. They looked forward to seeing me, and I looked forward to seeing them. So I decided to do something a little out of the ordinary.

There was a taco joint nearby. Every few weeks, around midnight, I would buy tacos for every employee. You should've seen the looks on their faces—those tacos always provided a much-needed break and a sense of relief at being served after serving others all day.

So why did I spend my money on tacos for every employee? Because I wanted them to know that I simply cared about them. Let's fast-forward several more months:

By this point, every employee at the time knew who I was. Every waitress, waiter, bouncer, manager, etc. If I wasn't there for a week or so, I would get text messages asking where I was.

Whenever I spent time with them, I asked genuine questions, we would get to talk about life. I intentionally invested in them, and they knew how much I genuinely cared about them.

One evening, the fruit of my generosity produced. I had stayed up late, just talking to employees and strangers as I usually would.

Then one employee came up to me and said, "What's your deal?"

"What?" I asked, confused.

"You come in here all the time, you are so nice, you bring us free tacos, you give audacious-sized tips, you stay up late and even offer to help clean for free. Why are you like this? What's your deal?"

I just laughed and said, "I just love you all. And I love you all, because I have first been so loved."

And right then, after almost a year of investing in these people, we shared in a conversation about grace, love, mercy, Jesus, the Church, Christianity, and they listened to the Gospel presented with open minds and hearts.

People Want To Know That You _____

That employee did *not* like Christians. They believed Christians were hateful, judgmental, close-minded, and more. So what made me different from all the other people who claimed to be a Christian?

It's simple: they knew I cared.

> People want to know that you care before they want to know what you care about.

That's a big mistake Christians make when sharing their faith: they tell people what they care about *before* the other person understands that Christians actually care about them as a person.

This is why arguments via social media never go well. The lack of a personal relationship immediately sets you up for failure. Telling others what you care about before showing them that you care will only contribute to that negative list of things people will think of when they hear the word "Christian."

Jesus was a great example of what it means to show people that you care *before* telling them what He cared about. One time, for example, Jesus was invited over to a tax collector's house to eat and chill.

This tax collector's name was Matthew, and he later wrote down this event in a letter that we refer to in the Bible as the Gospel According to Matthew (or the Book of Matthew).

The ancient Jewish community despised tax collectors because they represented the interests of the Romans, the nation actively oppressing Israel at the time. But it wasn't just tax collectors who gathered at Matthew's house.

> "Later, Matthew invited Jesus and his disciples to his home
> as dinner guests, along with many tax collectors and other
> disreputable sinners. But when the Pharisees saw this, they
> asked his disciples, "Why does your teacher eat with such
> scum?" (Matthew 9:10-11 NLT)

Notice how it says "and other disreputable sinners." Who were they? To help you better understand, try to envision them as the people you wouldn't like. You know who they are.

Jesus spent his time investing in these people—people whom others didn't like or even outright hated. He was invited because they believed He cared about them, and because of that, they wanted to know what He cared about.

Jesus also preached the Good News and made it a point to teach them. He had a firm conviction of what He believed in. Not long after, He even uses the language to say that His new friends are like people with an illness and He is the doctor.

So don't think you have to sacrifice your convictions to make friends with those who would disagree with you. Rather, if you want other people to know what you care about, you first need to demonstrate that you care about them.

So what are you doing to show others that you care? Are you tipping your waiters and waitresses? Tip well, because they remember. (I'm talking specifically to you, Sunday after-church crowd.) Are you being consistent in the lives of other people who you want to see know Jesus?

I pray I can always be the type of person who shows others that he cares *before* sharing his opinion. I hope I can be the person who gets invited to lunch parties by people with diverse lifestyles and beliefs, because those people know I genuinely care about them.

Whatever you do, don't tell others what you care about unless you have first proven to them that you care about them. If you want to do that well, your starting point has to be from a place of loving Jesus. Otherwise, you'll just be doing this in your own power and strength, and it won't be nearly as successful.

Let everything you are and everything you do start and revolve around loving Jesus. Sit back and reflect on God's love for you, and then let that love influence your love for Him.

Let His love inspire a desire to know who God is as a person. To know what He likes, know what He loves. More importantly, to know who He loves. The more we understand how much God loves people, the more we will share His love.

The more we share God's love for people, we will naturally want to show God our love by doing what makes Him happy: loving Him and loving others. The closer you are to God, the greater your love for people will be.

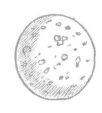

REFLECTION QUESTIONS

1. According to Jesus, what is the Gospel? (See Mark 1:15)

2. Has there ever been a time in your life that you felt you were irredeemable, that you were too far-gone? How does it make you feel to know you are not too far-gone? To know that there is good news: Jesus simply loves you.

3. God loves people. Why is it important for us to really think about this and understand it?

4. "People want to know you care before they want to know what you care about." How can you apply this idea to your life?

5. What does it mean to simply love Jesus?

CHAPTER

FIVE

THE MORE I SEEK JESUS,
THE MORE I NEED JESUS

"What is my purpose?" I've asked that question many times, and I'm sure you have as well. Everyone wants to know what their purpose is, and everyone wants to know that their life has purpose.

Here's some good news: you have a purpose, and it's simpler than you'd think it is:

To love God with everything you have so that you can love others and prepare the world for when Jesus returns.

When Jesus launched His ministry, He went around teaching and proclaiming the "Good News" (the Gospel). But what is the "Good News?" Often when preachers reference the Gospel, they're usually referring to the life, death, and resurrection of Jesus.

While that may be true, I'm not so certain it is *just* that. Jesus's resurrection was indeed good news, and by believing in Him, it is true that we find abundant and eternal life. (John 3:16, 10:10.)

But if the Gospel was exclusively about Jesus, how is it that even before He died, Jesus was claiming to preach the Gospel? He hadn't even been resurrected, yet He claimed to be preaching the Good News.

"...Jesus came into Galilee, proclaiming the gospel (Good News) of God, and saying, 'The time is fulfilled, and the kingdom of God is at hand; repent and believe in the gospel.'" (Mark 1:14b-15 ESV, parenthesis added)

According to Jesus, the Good News is that God's Kingdom

is near. Even if we back up a little bit, you will notice that those who wrote about the life of Jesus also recognized that Jesus's mission started way before He was born. Look at the opening words of the book of Mark (the first of the four gospels written):

> "This is the Good News about Jesus the Messiah, the Son of God. It (the Good News) began just as the prophet Isaiah had written: "Look, I am sending my messenger ahead of you, and he will prepare your way. (Malachi 3:1)
>
> He is a voice shouting in the wilderness, 'Prepare the way for the LORD's coming! Clear the road for him! (Isaiah 40:3)'" (Mark 1:1-3 NLT, parentheses added)

You may recall how in the last chapter we referenced Isaiah's proclamation to the people of Israel that they were not too far-gone, that God will never turn His back on His people.

With that proclamation, Isaiah foretold and promised that God's Kingdom would come soon. But even by going back to Isaiah, the issues Isaiah addresses take us even further back...

To the beginning.

In The Beginning...

We talked about what happened *in the beginning* before, but I want us to go back and revisit it, to see it from a slightly different angle, because it is key to fully understanding our purpose.

That's the beautiful thing about the Scriptures: you can always go back and see something new. Especially after you pick up on a theme to follow.

In the beginning, God desired for us to have a relationship with Him. Creation began with God creating a pair: Heaven and Earth. Many other pairs followed: The day and the night, the land and the sea, the sun and the moon, the animals belonging to the sky and the animals belonging to the land.

The last pair that God made is the pinnacle of His Creation, man and woman— humanity.

After God makes all of these pairs, what happens next? The *two* become *one*. (Genesis 2:24) I don't believe this was a coincidence. I believe this was by design; it was intentional.

I believe if this were a painting, if God was working a brush on a canvas and we asked what He was working on, He would say, "*One.*"

God's desire from the beginning was that all of Heaven and Earth, God and humanity, would exist in perfect relationship, that all of Creation would be one. This was symbolized by man and woman becoming one.

But then what happens? Humanity is deceived. Evil enters the world, and the *one* is severed into *two*, separated. Heaven and Earth were split apart.

Ever since that moment, God's goal was to make this right, for the two to become one again. Heaven and Earth, God and us. How does that happen?

The wedge has to be removed.

A wedge is some type of material that is driven between two objects or parts of an object to secure or separate them.

When I was in high school, I really enjoyed chopping wood. Maybe it's an overcompensation for my theatrical personality, but there's something about the hard labor of using an axe to chop firewood that I find both masculine and enjoyable.

While I prefer the most primitive method of chopping wood, occasionally I would use the support of a wedge. It was a piece of metal with one side tapered down.

I would use a sledgehammer to drive that wedge into a large chunk of wood and split it. That made it easier for my axe to split the rest of the wood into smaller pieces for great firewood.

While a wedge is a great wood-chopping tool, isn't it similar to what's happened to our world? Selfishness entered the world when Adam and Eve were deceived and disobeyed God.

Thus, by choosing to trust in the power of *me*, humanity drove the hammer on the wedge of evil, splitting Heaven and Earth apart. As long as that wedge remains, our world will continue to be broken.

As we've talked about before, this wasn't a one-time event or a one-time issue. That occurrence may have been the source, but the result of that wedge still affects us to this very day. Everything wrong we see in the world and in our personal lives is because of that wedge.

It's that wedge that causes prejudice, racism, and pride. Greed, abuse, lust, and envy. Depression and anxiety, though they do not make a person "evil," are deep and heavy burdens that would not exist were it not for that wedge.

When you lose your temper and say mean things to other people. When you're stressed out and desperate because of the balance on your bank account. When you lay in your bed, tears slipping from your eyes, because there's this deep, tight, aching emptiness that drips into your soul, tricking you into believing that no one truly loves you.

These, and everything else that is broken and wrong in this world, are caused by this wedge.

So how can this problem be fixed? Simple: by removing the wedge. When selfishness and evil is removed from this world, all that is wrong will be made right.

But how can we, as inherently selfish people, remove the sin problem in this world?

The answer is that *we* can't.

The Third Step

The next step of learning to simply love Jesus is understanding that *the more I seek Jesus, the more I need Jesus.*

All of us have the same problem. We all feel the need to overcome our issues and the issues around us with *our* strength, by the power of *me.*

This includes removing the wedge of sin that separates us from Heaven, even if we're unaware that we're trying to do it. An attempt to create a better world, a pocket of Eden... isn't this why governments are formed?

When we have a personal struggle or a problem, and someone offers their help, what do we say?

"It's my problem, *I'll* fix it."

How far does that get us? When we take our problems into our hands, they usually just get worse. We get more stressed out, more overwhelmed, more out of control.

So how do we fix the problems in our personal lives if *we* are the problem?

Simply love Jesus.

What have we learned so far? That Jesus simply loves us. When we truly realize how much He loves us, it will inspire us to love Him, to know who He is as a person.

So we pray, and we dive into the Scriptures to learn who He is and who He loves. This inspires us to see other people as God sees them, and through that lens we will want to serve them.

These things lead to a revelation, which convinces us to shift our direction: keeping our eyes fixated on Jesus.

I really like how the *New International Version* translates Proverbs 29:18: "Where there is no revelation, people cast off restraint; but blessed is the one who heeds wisdom's instruction."

This proverb teaches that if people do not have a purpose (or a *revelation*, as the NIV translates this word), they run aimlessly and go in any direction, even the one that leads to brokenness.

But people are set apart from the rest of the world if they heed the instruction that comes from the Scriptures (or wisdom, as is translated in NIV.)

I believe everyone wants to know what direction their life is going. We want to know that our life is not for nothing, to know that we were born for a reason.

This is why we value social media so much, right? To know that our lives are seen by others, to know that we are not forgotten.

Everyone desires direction, even if you want to live in the moment and go where the wind may carry. In *The Fellowship of the Ring,* J.R.R. Tolkien famously wrote, "Not all those who wander are lost."

Many who want to wander do so for adventure, exploration, or curiosity, but therein lies their own revelation which gives direction: their direction is to live life open-handedly and set their mind to having loose expectations.

When you have a revelation, you get struck with a new idea that changes the way you think.

When you change what you think, you will change the way you live.

A revelation will shift your life in a new direction.

When you change
what you think, you
will change the way
you live.

If a new mother holds her newborn in her hands for the first time and she is struck with love for her child, then her revelation is that she is now a mother. When that revelation strikes her, the direction of her life shifts. The way she lives revolves around and is filtered by this revelation that she's a mother.

Isn't this how it ought to be with Jesus? I know it's tempting to just keep reading, but consider putting this book down for a moment and just think about that.

Isn't this how it should be in our relationship with Jesus? To have a revelation about who Jesus is and shift the direction of our lives because of that newfound revelation giving us purpose?

Fix Your Eyes On Jesus

When Jesus started His ministry, He set out to find disciples. A disciple, in this context, is someone who is being mentored by a teacher on their relationship with God. In Jesus's day, when you committed to being a disciple, you would devote your *entire life* to following your teacher.

You would leave your job, your home, and everything else behind and literally follow your Rabbi. It was the art of imitation; your goal was to become exactly like your teacher.

You wanted to teach as they taught, think as they thought, all for the purpose of growing in your relationship with God through their wisdom and understanding of who God is and what the Scriptures mean.

Near the beginning of Jesus's ministry, he happens upon some fishers. Average, ordinary young people. Jesus approaches these fishers and performs a miracle. In a single moment, simply by instructing them to throw their nets on the other side of their boat, he helps them catch so many fish that it would have made them instantly rich.

But rather than focus on how much money they could have made, the fishermen have a revelation. This revelation causes them to change the direction of their life.

> "When Simon Peter realized what had happened, he fell to his knees before Jesus and said, "Oh, Lord, please leave me— I'm such a sinful man." For he was awestruck by the number of fish they had caught, as were the others with him. His partners, James and John, the sons of Zebedee, were also amazed. Jesus replied to Simon, 'Don't be afraid! From now on you'll be fishing for people!' And as soon as they landed, they left everything and followed Jesus." (Luke 5:8-11 NLT)

Jesus wants the same for you. It won't be easy, but it is simple: Follow Him.

Jesus said, "Whoever wants to be my disciple must deny themselves and take up their cross daily and follow me. For whoever wants to save their life will lose it, but whoever loses their life for me will save it." (Luke 9:23 NIV)

So that's what they did; they followed their Rabbi. They wanted to know God just as Jesus knew Him, to teach as Jesus taught, to walk as He walked, to do what He does.

Later, Peter had a unique experience, and I believe it teaches us a powerful lesson about overcoming our problems.

Jesus's disciples were in a boat on the Sea of Galilee, and a big storm overtook them. They were all terrified, which should indicate the kind of disaster they were facing. If professional fishermen (who worked on the water for a living) were scared of a storm, how scary *was* this storm? Must've been pretty bad!

But in the midst of the storm, they literally saw Jesus walking on the water. The very chaos that terrified the disciples had no choice but to obey the authority of Jesus.

Why would the wind and the waves obey Jesus? What kind

of presence would person-less winds and waters obey? There's only one presence they would find familiar: that of the one who spoke them into existence *in the beginning.*

Peter wanted to know if it's really Jesus walking on the waters, so He called out to Jesus that if it was *really* Him then He should tell Peter to come out onto the water with Him.

Why in the world would Peter think he could walk on water? Because he's a disciple. In Peter's mind, if his Rabbi walks on water, then he should walk on water because disciples are to be like their Rabbi.

So what happens? Jesus calls out to Peter, and Peter actually begins to walk on the water and take steps towards Jesus!

But then something changes, he begins to sink into the water and Jesus has to save Him. Why? I love that the Scriptures are so detailed in this part, because it gives us an abundantly clear reason.

> "So Peter went over the side of the boat and walked on the water toward Jesus. *But when he saw the strong wind and the waves*, he was terrified and began to sink. 'Save me, Lord!' he shouted." (Matthew 14:29-30 NLT, emphasis added)

Peter was walking on the stormy waters, waves crashing all around him, and where was he walking? Toward Jesus! He had his eyes fixed on Jesus. With every step, his eyes were focused on Jesus. The moment he began to sink was the moment he took his eyes *off* of Jesus!

When he saw the winds and the waves, it became about "Peter's power." The winds and the waves were too overwhelming for Peter. He wasn't strong enough in his own strength.

The closer Peter stepped toward Jesus, the more reliant he was on Jesus to sustain him. The only way Peter could walk on water is when he kept his eyes on Jesus and when Jesus was the only direction of his steps.

The same is true for us. The answer to walking through the storms in your life is to keep your eyes fixed on Jesus. As the Scriptures also say,

"Therefore, since we have so great a cloud of witnesses surrounding us, let us also lay aside every encumbrance and the sin which so easily entangles us, and let us run with endurance the race that is set before us, fixing our eyes on Jesus, the author and perfecter of faith, who for the joy set before Him endured the cross, despising the shame, and has sat down at the right hand of the throne of God."

(Hebrews 12:1-2 NASB)

When we look at the wind and the waves, it's about our power and our strength. It's about control. But when we relinquish control, we find victory. As the Scriptures say, "...when I am weak, then I am strong." (2 Cor. 12:10)

Let me say it another way: When we try to control the waters, our feet will sink. But when we keep our eyes on Jesus and let Him be the one who controls our storms, we find firm footing.

The more we seek Jesus, the more we need Jesus. The more I see just how broken and how overwhelming the darkness is, the more aware I am that He's not just the light of the world, but the light of *my* world. And I *need* my light if I'm going to walk through the darkness.

Will you allow yourself to need Jesus, to be the light to your dark world?

I don't mean we can or should ignore the wind and the waves. Peter was very aware he was in the middle of a storm. But we shouldn't give it attention it doesn't deserve.

Rather, we should live in the tension, resisting the temptation to try to take control, and instead give control to Jesus by fixing our eyes on Him and walking toward Him, all while trusting that He will handle the storm.

The same is true for the problems in our world. I know it may seem counter-productive, but the answer to the issues in our world is not to take control, but to *relinquish* control.

Not that we are passive and should do nothing, but rather we are *choosing* not to draw upon our own wisdom or the strength to overcome the issues in our world. Instead, we rely on those things from God.

Have you not heard the words of "The Heavenly Wisdom" (1918)?

Turn your eyes upon Jesus,
Look full in His wonderful face;
And the things of earth will grow strangely dim
In the light of His glory and grace.

We are not to be passive; we are supposed to take action, or else we cannot truly love God. Don't forget that the closer you are to God, the greater your love for people will grow. And the greater your love for people, the more instinctual it will be to serve and care for them.

When I was nineteen, I lived in downtown Chicago, Illinois. While there, I spent time serving the homeless. I can't begin to tell you how many people I interacted with during the time that I lived there. But among the many memories, my experience with a man named Tom stands out the most.

I attended a few churches while living in Chicago. Every time I walked down West Chicago Avenue, I'd walk past this one McDonald's.

Tom would often sit near the McDonald's. Every time I saw him there, I would buy him lunch. We would sit down and talk about life, faith, and everything in between.

After lunch, I would give him whatever dollars I had in my pocket. I would never just buy him food; I would always give him money afterward. Why? Because Jesus said to never refuse someone who would borrow from you, and always give to those who beg. (Matt. 5:42.)

After several months, he chose to follow Jesus. It wasn't because of my money; it was because he knew I cared about him. Because of this, he was open to hear what I cared about.

I didn't need to put thought into whether I would serve and care for that awesome man; I just did it. I did it because I have a desire for every person to find the same joy and excitement I have found in Christ.

To know the length, the width, the height, and the depth of God's love is to see God's Kingdom. Because when I understand the depths of His love, I not only see the world for how divided it really is, but also as it should be: renewed, remade, and restored through Christ's sacrifice.

Answering God's Prayers?

I often wonder if it's possible to answer God's prayers. We ask for God to answer our prayers, but what do we do when God prays?

I don't have an answer for that, but oftentimes in the gospels, Jesus prays to the Father and asks for something. I find that fascinating.

One of his most compelling prayers took place when Jesus prayed that we would be *one*.

> "I am praying not only for these disciples but also for all who will ever believe in me through their message. I pray that they will all be one, just as you and I are one—as you are in me, Father, and I am in you. And may they be in us so that the world will believe you sent me.
>
> I have given them the glory you gave me, so they may be one as we are one. I am in them and you are in me. May they experience such perfect unity that the world will know that you sent me and that you love them as much as you love me." (John 17:21-23 NLT)

There are so many implications within this prayer that we could talk about, but I want to focus on Jesus's desire that everyone who would ever believe in Him would be *one*.

How is that even possible? How in the world could we be one *just as* Jesus and the Father are one, especially with how broken and divisive we are? We would have to love each other perfectly. We would have to be completely selfless.

It's almost like we would have to be Jesus. But we can't be Jesus... right?

On one hand, we can't be the person Jesus, God the Son. But, on the other hand, and in the most non-blasphemous way possible, we *can*.

After Jesus left Earth, He promised to send us a helper: the Holy Spirit. What separates a person who truly loves Jesus and someone who does not is that God's Spirit becomes *one* with that person.

What does the Spirit do? The Spirit empowers us the same way the Spirit empowered Jesus. The Spirit helps us in our weaknesses. (Rom. 8:26.) And what are our weaknesses? Our selfish nature, our *me*-focused mentality.

The Spirit empowers us to obediently carry out the will of the Father, just as Jesus was obedient to carrying out His Father's will. And it was Jesus's prayer that you and I would be one, that we would have perfect unity.

(It's interesting that, to me, Jesus's desire seems to tie back to what we talked about *in the beginning*.)

In order for us to be one as Jesus desires and prayed for, we need to rely on God to make that possible. It's like I've been saying: The more I seek Jesus, the more I need Jesus. But how, then, do we rely on the Spirit to be our strength?

Love God with everything you have.

Love God with all your heart, soul, mind, and strength.

It always, always, always, should come back to the bestest commandment (Deut. 6:5, Lev. 19:18).

With all of your everything, love Jesus. Love God with everything you have, *so that* you can love others and prepare the world for when Jesus returns.

Who's Your Plus One?

How do we prepare the world for when Jesus returns? I view it like a wedding, and I believe that, in a way, Jesus does, too.

Weddings are exciting, a time filled with celebration. Even in 1st Century Israel, weddings were exciting. Jesus uses weddings as illustrations on multiple occasions. He even refers to Himself as the bridegroom in Scripture.

> "One day the disciples of John the Baptist came to Jesus and asked him, 'Why don't your disciples fast like we do and the Pharisees do?'
>
> Jesus replied, 'Do wedding guests mourn while celebrating with the groom? Of course not. But someday the groom will be taken away from them, and then they will fast.'" (Matthew 9:14-15 NLT)

The practice of fasting, according to the Bible, is to deprive your body of what it needs for a period of time in order to draw closer to God and let Him fill our needs. It's a strenuous process. But when being questioned about fasting, Jesus uses a wedding as an illustration and says He is the groom.

This illustration of a wedding is used many times throughout the Bible; it's a theme. To better understand why this theme is important, let me explain to you how weddings worked in first-century Israel.

Back then, dating as we know it today didn't exist. If a guy and a girl liked each other they wouldn't go to the nearest Starbucks and chat about their fancy new camel. They may have some social interactions, but if there was enough attraction or interest, then the man would propose a marriage to the woman's father.

If they were to be married, then they would enter betrothal. A betrothal is a period of time before the wedding ceremony. The couple would be legally married, but the groom would go and prepare a home for him and his wife, and a wedding ceremony would be prepared.

The bride and groom wouldn't see each other during betrothal, and the bride would wait for the groom to return, where they would then go to the wedding ceremony. The entire wedding would last about three weeks, and it was a massive party.

Lots of ceremonial traditions. Guests from all over would attend. Lots of partying, lots of eating, lots of music and drinks and dancing. It was a good time.

In fact, Jesus's first miracle took place at a wedding. They had run out of wine, and His first miracle was keeping the party going by turning water into wine.

Do you remember what Jesus said in Matthew 9:14-15? "Do wedding guests mourn while celebrating with the groom? Of course not. But someday the groom will be taken away from them, and then they will fast."

Jesus illustrates Himself as the groom. Three days after dying, He rose from the grave, and then after forty days, He ascended to Heaven. The Groom was taken away.

Jesus has promised that one day, He will return. He even uses the same language as the betrothal in John 14:1-4.

"Don't let your hearts be troubled. Trust in God, and trust also in me. There is more than enough room in my Father's home. If this were not so, would I have told you that I am going to prepare a place for you? When everything is ready, I will come and get you, so that you will always be with me where I am. And you know the way to where I am going."

When Jesus died and rose again, that was the betrothal. Just like a groom, He is going to prepare a place in His father's house. But if Jesus is the groom, who is the bride?

Us.

We are the bride.

In the Bible, the church is referred to as the Bride of Christ. (Eph. 5:29-32.)

Jesus left, but just like the groom, He is coming back. As one of Jesus's disciples wrote:

"Then I saw a new heaven and a new earth, for the first heaven and the first earth had passed away, and the sea was no more. And I saw the holy city, a new Jerusalem, coming down out of heaven from God, prepared as a bride adorned for her husband." (Revelation 21:1-2)

"And the angel said to me, 'Write this: Blessed are those who are invited to the marriage supper of the Lamb.' And he said to me, 'These are the true words of God.'" (19:9)

Do you know what this means? This means that we're a big wedding party! And the joy is that you get to treat everyone, Christian or not, like you'd invite someone to a wedding.

Whenever I'm attending a wedding, I get asked if I'm bringing someone with me—a "plus one."

Do you know what I *don't* do when inviting someone to a wedding? I don't yell at them angrily, try to scare them to go to the wedding, or shame them until they agree.

Awkward, right? Yet there are people who act like this in the Church (though I doubt they are truly Christians).

When I invite someone to a wedding, it's fun and exciting. I'm happy that I can invite them! We should be reaching others for God's Kingdom like this.

People are attracted to what they're missing out on. Are you living your life in a way that teaches others they're missing out on something if they don't have Jesus?

That's what will catch others' attention. And that's what will be effective when sending invitations for others to be our "plus one."

So who will be your plus one? And will you live out your purpose as your means of inviting others?

Our purpose is to love God with everything we have so we can love others and prepare the world for when Jesus returns. And when He does, everything is going to be different. Revelations 21:1-4 (NLT) says this:

> "Then I saw a new heaven and a new earth, for the old heaven and the old earth had disappeared. And the sea was also gone. And I saw the holy city, the new Jerusalem, coming down from God out of heaven like a bride beautifully dressed for her husband.
>
> I heard a loud shout from the throne, saying, 'Look, God's home is now among his people! He will live with them, and they will be his people. God himself will be with them. He will wipe every tear from their eyes, and there will be no more death or sorrow or crying or pain. All these things are gone forever.'"

One day, everything will be made right.

One day, all the tears in your life will be wiped away.

One day, all the brokenness will be gone, and the world will be beautiful again.

That day is coming soon, but we have to work now and hurry because Jesus is returning.

And when He does, we're going to have a *massive* party.

REFLECTION
QUESTIONS

1. What does the word "Gospel" mean?

2. "The more I seek Jesus, the more I need Jesus." What does this mean to you?

3. Have you ever thought of Jesus returning like a big wedding celebration? How does it change the way you feel Christians should be sharing their faith with others?

4. People are naturally attracted to whatever they're missing out on. Are you living your life in a way that teaches others they're missing out on something if they don't have Jesus?

5. What does it mean to simply love Jesus?

CHAPTER SIX

What does it mean to (S)imply love Jesus?

D o you think God has faith in us?

    We talk a lot about us believing in God, but what about God having faith in us?

I mean, when we take a look around the state of our world, it can seem a bit overwhelming. When something is overwhelming, it drains our joy. And without joy, hope is increasingly difficult to find.

Maybe you feel you need some hope as well.

This world also needs that hope right now, too. That's not going to change because of who the President is. It's not going to change because of one church or a gifted speaker. This world doesn't need some kind of loud spiritual awakening.

The world needs Jesus working through *you*.

I believe God wants to empower you to be a light in your home, in your neighborhood. God wants to give *you* the strength to move mountains, the power to love your neighbors so well that they realize they're missing out on something if they don't have what you have.

When that happens, you get to tell them that it's not anything special about you but rather the power that works through you, and that power has a name, and His name is Jesus!

I don't think Jesus would've left unless God believed we had what it took, through Christ, to complete the purpose He set before us. When Jesus left Earth, He promised He would send His followers the Holy Spirit to empower God's people to prepare the world for when He returns.

Here's how it happened...

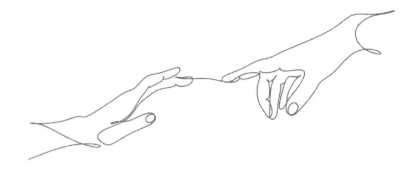

The world needs
Jesus working
through you.

The Spirit Didn't Stop Working

As instructed, the followers of Jesus waited in Jerusalem, Israel around the year 33$^{AD(CE)}$. On the night of Pentecost, a Jewish holiday dating back long before Jesus's arrival on Earth, the Spirit of God descended down and empowered Jesus's followers.

This special supernatural empowerment helped them to boldly and obediently carry out the will of the Father through the power of the Holy Spirit. They spread the Good News of Jesus's resurrection and God's Kingdom.

Every single day after that, the Church grew. Acts 2:42 (NIV) says that they "devoted themselves to the apostles' teaching and to fellowship, to the breaking of bread and to prayer."

The Church grew, and then they faced persecution, which scattered them. But even as they ran from persecution, they could not stop talking about Jesus and how God had transformed their lives.

They spread the Church from Judea to Samaria and all throughout the known world. And even when the world as we knew it expanded, the Gospel continued to spread. No matter how much persecution the Church sustained, they continued to grow and push forward.

Why? Because they had their eyes fixed on Jesus, and they kept running after Him. They kept loving God with all of their everything, making it impossible not to love their neighbor and serve others, even their enemies.

God wants to do the same through you. The Spirit doesn't stop working. Even though things haven't been perfect in the past, that doesn't have to be the case in the future. Together, we can work to prepare the world for when Jesus returns.

And if it seems overwhelming, that's okay, because trusting in God means accepting that we cannot do these things in our own strength.

Because the more we seek Jesus, the more that we need Jesus.

The Last Step

But the more we seek Jesus, the more we are reminded of the Good News that He is returning soon. Our strength is rejuvenated, because when Jesus comes back, all that is wrong will be made right. Soon there will be a day where Heaven and Earth are no longer separated, that wedge will be removed.

On that day, all of your struggles, all of your burdens, all of the problems in your life and in our world will pass away.

Every tear will be wiped away, every hurt will be healed, and all selfishness and evil will be contained outside of the New Heaven and New Earth. There will be nothing that pollutes our world or our hearts.

There will be no more countries, no more wars, no more flags, no more racism, no more hatred. All people will be equally loved and equally loving. These things are coming soon, and it's our responsibility to prepare the world for the triumphant return.

The way we prepare this world comes back to that bestest command: *To love God with everything you have so that you can love others (and prepare the world for when Jesus returns.)*

God wants to empower you to shift your eyes from what's wrong with other people and instead keep your eyes fixated on Jesus, who gave up His life for all people.

God wants to empower you to see that true strength is not holding on, but *letting go*. To follow in the footsteps of Jesus and give up our life for others, to sacrifice ourselves in service to loving others with all of our heart.

This is how we take the words of Jesus seriously. He said that those who try to find their life will lose it, but those who lose their life for Jesus will find it. (Matt. 10:39 ESV)

But being empowered by God requires you to share the kind of intimate relationship with Him where the gates of your heart are wide open.

The rivers of living water must flow freely through that gate straight to your soul, and those waters must fill you. The overflow of those waters must pour out onto the world around you.

To be empowered by God requires that kind of relationship from you; it requires you to *know* Him. But to know Him, as a person, requires you to have this longing within you.

This kind of longing can only come from the stillness we find in green pastures or when sitting beside quiet waters. And in the stillness, we reflect, and we come to a revelation of His love for us:

The kind of love that would lay its own life down so we would realize the chains of our own brokenness. The kind of love that, when we were wrestling under the covers with our own selfishness, chose to lay its life down as the ultimate symbol of forgiveness.

The kind of love that offers the hand of acceptance, calling us to lay down with Him in the grave, allowing evil to exhaust its strength on Him. And then, after three days, we might walk out of the grave with this kind of love to live a new and resurrected life.

To know Him requires you to have the longing and desire for Him that is gifted to you when you have a revelation of this kind of love.

You have to let God's love for you influence your love for Him, and you have to let His love overflow out of you and on to the world.

To find this revelation, you have to enter into His sanctuary, where you can meditate on the glorious destiny of His love. Truly, God is good to those whose hearts are pure and love Him.

To enter into this sanctuary, I challenge you to take one last step, the fourth movement in this idea, which is to ask one question.

Ask it again, and again, and again.

It's a question that sparks the never-ending cycle that this idea revolves around.

"What does it mean to simply love Jesus?"

Simply Love Jesus

And so, here we are. We've reached the end of this journey. Or at least for right now. Simply love Jesus is a philosophy, one that continues to change the way you think and challenge the way you live.

It's not something you experience once, you re-experience it. That's why this book was designed for you to re-read. Regardless, I hope this journey has been kind to you.

I wonder what would happen if you went back to chapter one and read the summary I gave you for *Simply Love Jesus*. Would it make more sense to you?

I believe in the power of good questions. The impetus for this book was a really good question that changed my life.

Your journey is not the same as mine, but I pray that this question has blessed you as it has blessed me and my faith journey. It changed the way I see people. It breathed new air into the way I understand truth. It opened my eyes to something beautiful.

Simply Love Jesus is the idea that everything in life should start and revolve around loving Jesus. I believe this idea can breathe life into the movement of Christianity that was started over two thousand years ago.

It's a beautiful question because it's not about teaching something new; it's about bringing many of us back to something very old, the greatest commandment: To love God with all of your heart, soul, mind, and strength. And to love your neighbor as yourself. All of Scripture rests on this "bestest command."

It is my mission and purpose to teach others the meaning of that good question. I invite you to join me in the journey of sharing what it means to simply love Jesus with others.

Infinitely more important, behind that good question is the simple desire for all of us to love Jesus and to share God's Kingdom with others. I believe this idea is one way to do that.

What do you think the world would look like if everyone chose to simply love Jesus? I think, at the least, the world would see Christians the way God intended them to be seen.

I think the Church would be healthier than it has ever been. I believe many people who were once "burned" by the church would come back and receive the transformational love of Jesus.

I believe that if everyone chose to simply love Jesus, we would be doing a great job at preparing this world for when Jesus returns.

At the beginning of this chapter, I asked a question:

"Do you think God has faith in us?"

I think He does. I believe God has allowed you to have the story you have so far because He knows you have the power, through Christ, to persevere through it.

I believe God has faith in you to trust in Him, to love Him, to love others, to be a good and faithful follower of Jesus. I know I have faith in you. And yes, that's probably a little easy to say considering I'm just writing some words on a page!

But... I do. Really and truly, I do.

In my dreams, or when I look at the beautiful blue sky, I have faith. In my mind and in my heart, I believe that Jesus will do great things through His followers.

I have faith in you.

I have faith and hope for the Church.

I have hope for a great big beautiful tomorrow.

Benediction

It all starts with you. It starts with your decision to simply love Jesus.

I pray that God will give you the courage and the strength to let go of the struggles you're holding on to.

I pray he'll grant you the strength to trust in Him, to keep your eyes fixed on Him. To let Him be your Good Shepherd who will lead you *through* your dark valley to green pastures and quiet waters.

I pray you will trust in Him to not only be the light of *the* world but also the light of *your* world. I pray that you will draw your wisdom and strength from the Holy Spirit, who will give you the power to love your neighbor.

I pray that He will give you the power to be quick to listen, slow to speak, and slow to get angry. For human anger does not produce the righteousness of God. (James 1:19)

I pray that God will help you to persevere through your trials, to count them as joy because they are producing more endurance within you. (James 1:2-3) I pray that you will remember in the midst of dark seasons that Jesus has overcome the world. (John 16:33)

I pray that you will remember that nothing in all of Creation can separate you from the love of God (Romans 8:39), and that you will grasp the width and length, height, and the depth of God's love. (Ephesians 3:18)

I pray that all of us who follow Jesus, regardless of denomination, will be *one*, just as Jesus and the Father are one. That we will have harmony even where there is theological diversity.

I pray that the Lord will bless you and keep you; I pray that the Lord will make his face shine on you and be gracious to you; I pray that the Lord will turn his face of favor toward you and give you peace. (Numbers 6:24-26)

I pray for the people who need God the most, but I pray most especially for the people who feel like they need Him the least.

I pray God will encourage you,

I pray God will comfort you,

I pray that God will empower you...

...and that you would be reminded that Jesus simply loves you.

Grace be upon you, peace be with you,
and may you walk in love.

@sljministries
https://simplylovejesus.com

CHAPTER SEVEN

And on the seventh day, God rested... (Genesis 2:2)

AFTERWORD

When we started this journey, I said that simply love Jesus is the idea that everything should start and revolve around loving Jesus. When you get to the last step, you start over and go through the whole process all over again.

That's what it means to live this lifestyle. When we are faced with a struggle or hardship in our life or in our world, finding the answer starts by asking that beautiful question: "What does it mean to simply love Jesus?"

That being said, to continue reading, please turn to Chapter 2.

STAY CONNECTED

Would you like me to come and speak at your church, conference, or event? You can get in contact with me by sending an email to caleb@simplylovejesus.com or simply sending me a text message to (678) 350-5957.

To stay connected to Simply Love Jesus™ Ministries, you can subscribe to our YouTube channel by searching for "Simply Love Jesus" or by following our Simply Love Jesus Podcast (available on iTunes, Spotify, and more.)

As a ministry, Simply Love Jesus™ exists to influence and inspire all people to live a life that starts and revolves around loving Jesus. We create content and resources for young adults designed to simplify the complicated issues of life and faith.

If you want to join the Simply Love Jesus community you can join our Facebook group by searching—you guessed it —"Simply Love Jesus."

You can find all of this by visiting our website,
www.simplylovejesus.com.
Follow us on Instagram @sljministries.

THANK YOU

This book took seven years to finish.

It was a long, *long,* journey. It felt like I kept hitting road-block after roadblock, putting this dream on pause. Because as long as something is a dream, it can't actually fail, right?

I cried, shouted with frustration, and procrastinated because of anxiety and fear. But if something only stays a dream, it will never have the chance to come true.

Now here we are, and I couldn't have reached this point if not for the emotional and financial support of others. From family to friends, mentors, and even strangers, thank you.

I am humbled by the people who have listened to the message that God called me to share and who were inspired to take part in that journey. I want to take a moment to thank those who went the extra mile to encourage me through this process, and those who were the first to step up with their generosity.

Special thanks to:

Amina "Tita" Buxo (Abuela)
Rafael "Papa" Buxo (Abuelo)
Marcia Davis (Mom)
Ken Davis (Dad)
Stephen Sapp
Aaron Collier
Brian Drinkwine
Justin Owens
Giovanna Gomez (Aunt)
Hubert Gomez (Uncle)
Joshua Davis (Brother)
Savannah Davis (Sister-In-Law)
Andrew Gomez (Cousin)
Alison Goedde
Rachel Robinson (Cousin)
Darian Robinson
Stephen Davis (Cousin)
Jerry Davis (Grandpa)
Nancy Davis (Grandma)
Shirley Stewart (Great Aunt)
Jacob Pearce
Griffin Stuart
Jacob Neu
Carson Tow
Micah Mayes
Sydney Bollback
Michael Boyle
Christopher Huling
Jason Bollback
Tim Lucken
Chuck & Andrea Byrge
Chaz Byrge
Marie Esther Leafblad

Jordan Rubin
Josh Salmonsen
Franchesca Salmonsen
Ryan Thompson
John Sevier
Reece Daniell
Johnny Taylor
Najee Daniels
Daniel Gray
Mike Haynes
Ty Hirsch
Lily Gallagher
Dawn & Chris Fegans
Leanne Garr
Ashley Camp
Kali Kramer
Leanne Chambless
Zulma Merced
Danine Winer
Sheila Woodruff
Jenny Esquivel
Carmen Nieves
Eileen Hehman
Andrea Fisher
Tim & Vicky Hamilton
Brooke Van Bruggen
Raianne Vasquez
Matt Timmons
Daytrian Hensen
Phillip Markert
Amy De Graaff
Spencer Reijgers
Nathaniel Young
Ben Wolf

Greg & Angela Towler
Caleb Towler
Beth & Frank Struck
Rex & Melanie Milburn
Heath & Resa Eckhart
Abhijeet Antin
Lou Martinez
Lisa Yancey
Kristin Gardner
Joseph Anderson
Juan Machado &
Romina Dalessandro
Carlos Torres
Malcolm Parks
Aneka Culp
Daniel & Amanda Cazenave
Joshua Dallas
Simi Lawoyin
Alan Pierce Jr.
Justin Kron
Teresa Gomez
Leah Colchado
Kristen Metzger
Kylee Barnard
Caroline Whitehead
Ben & Meredith Davis
Sergio Lopez-Galvan
Leslie Schleisman
Tracy Oeltjenbruns
Carmen Aranda
Cameron Furr
Tracey Howell
Will Mitchell

ABOUT THE AUTHOR

Rev. Caleb Davis is the Pioneer of Simply Love Jesus™ Ministries.

God placed a radical question on Caleb's heart: "What does it mean to simply love Jesus?"

Having already ministered to over a thousand students before graduating high school while pursuing a vision God had given him, Caleb considers that question one of the most life-changing things to ever happen to him. Since then, he focuses on teaching others the meaning behind this question.

With over ten years experience in student ministry, and as a former student pastor, Caleb yearns to reach young adults with the Good News. Even after formal education through Moody Bible Institute and informal education through personal study, he is still an eager student of theology.

Caleb and his twin brother, Joshua, were born in Orlando, Florida, to Ken and Marcia Davis. Caleb currently lives in Atlanta, Georgia. He is passionate about his Hispanic ethnicity from his mother's side of the family and his Scottish heritage from his father's side of the family. He loves Disney, philosophy, video games, music, movies, and tacos.

**To learn more about Caleb and his ministry,
visit www.simplylovejesus.com**

Made in the USA
Columbia, SC
10 November 2021